Texas

Lyda Hill, opposite, dedicates this book to the bold Texans everywhere who possess steadfast determination, audacious vision, and unwavering optimism that a diverse and industrious populace leads to a more prosperous tomorrow. Without losing sight of the state's rich history, these Texans demonstrate both the passion and the courage to dream big. The illustrious photographer Carol M. Highsmith captures the essence of this great state as only she can—in rich, vivid, and inspiring images certain to engage readers throughout Texas and beyond.

Texas, our Texas! All hail the mighty State!
Texas, our Texas! So wonderful so great!
Boldest and grandest, Withstanding ev'ry test;
O Empire wide and glorious, You stand supremely blest.
God bless you Texas! And keep you brave and strong,
That you may grow in power and worth,
Thro'out the ages long.

PHOTOGRAPHY BY CAROL M. HIGHSMITH

FEATURING IMAGES FROM THE LYDA HILL
TEXAS COLLECTION, LIBRARY OF CONGRESS

FOREWORD BY JAMES H. BILLINGTON

INTRODUCTION BY LONN TAYLOR

CHELSEA PUBLISHING, INC.,
IN ASSOCIATION WITH THE LIBRARY OF CONGRESS

FOREWORD

James H. Billington

IN THE COURSE of more than two centuries, the Library of Congress has become an incomparable custodian of our nation's memory and the largest and most inclusive repository anywhere of the world's recorded knowledge. The Library's pictorial collections alone represent an immense archive of the American experience.

This volume is an important installment in an ongoing major project of the Library of Congress to create a photographic record of early-twenty-first-century America, state by state. Housed in the Library, it will be available to people everywhere, copyright free.

Texas is drawn from the more than five thousand photographs that form the Lyda Hill Texas Collection of the Library of Congress—a permanent visual portrait of the exuberant, fast-changing state at the beginning of this century. The greatly gifted photographer Carol M. Highsmith spent six months producing a sweeping visual study of Texas, traveling and photographing a vast state as varied as the nation itself. She has captured the economic juggernaut that is the nation's second-largest state, from big cities to ghost towns, from the Gulf region's sparkling coastline to the awe-inspiring Big Bend mountains, from its rich artistic and cultural districts to its small-town treasures.

The collection intermixes the people, animals, and natural surroundings of Texas, as well as its independent spirit. These images are available on the Internet through the Library of Congress Prints and Photographs Online Catalog (*www.loc.gov/pictures/collection/highsm/*), free for downloading. The full Highsmith collection is one of the most popular in the Library's Prints and Photographs Division archive.

We are grateful to the philanthropist Lyda Hill for making possible this unique photographic study of Texas. The Hill families are longtime friends of the Library of Congress. We were honored to have had Lyda's mother, Margaret Hunt Hill, as a founding member of the Library's private-sector advisory group, the James Madison Council.

Texas is a vivid example of private support for a public institution. This book is an enduring contribution to the Library's growing record of our national life. We hope that you will enjoy exploring this inspiring and often dazzling depiction of the Lone Star State.

Although "the skies are not cloudy all day" in the parched Delaware Basin of far West Texas, roiling clouds mixed with sunshine are common. In these high desert surroundings beneath the Guadalupe Mountains, rainfall averages an inch a month. The range, which includes El Capitan—at 8,749 feet, the state's highest peak—stretches into New Mexico. The forbidding mountains were occupied by ancient Pueblo and Mogollon peoples and in the nineteenth century by the Apache and various Anglo outlaws.

INTRODUCTION

Lonn Taylor

THE FIRST THING that strikes visitors is the size of the state. It is 810 miles by automobile from Beaumont in the southeastern corner to El Paso on the western tip. It is 765 miles from Brownsville in the south to Amarillo in the Panhandle, and another 100 miles north from Amarillo to the Oklahoma state line. An old postcard from the 1930s shows a puzzled-looking couple in a roadster loaded with suitcases, contemplating a highway sign that reads "El Paso 500 miles." The caption below them says, "The sun has riz, the sun has set, / And here we is in Texas yet."

The distances are hard for easterners to grasp. When I was the director of a historic site in Round Top, a town in central Texas about halfway between Austin and Houston, I had a telephone call from a Boston friend, who explained that she was in Dallas for a few days and had a free afternoon and thought she would run down and see me. She gasped when I told her that it was a five-hour drive from Dallas to Round Top. "I could be in Canada if I drove five hours from Boston," she said. Texas is 400 square miles larger than France.

Bigness encompasses variety. It is almost impossible to generalize about Texas. The red clay and Piney Woods of East Texas might well be in Alabama; the high desert of the Big Bend is indistinguishable from Chihuahua. The Spanish moss and oak trees of the Coastal Bend, to which my grandmother Taylor's family immigrated in the 1820s, could be in the Mississippi Delta they left behind. My cousins there have little in common with the Spanish-speaking vaqueros of the Brush Country farther south, or with the hardscrabble German farmers of the Hill Country, or the drought-ridden ranchers of West Texas, who included my mother's people. Geographers distinguish eighteen physical regions of Texas.

In spite of its geographic variety, one quality is common to the entire state: vastness. Driving west on Interstate 20 from Fort Worth, the prairie rolls out in front of you to infinity, the sky above is bluer and bigger. Colonel Benjamin Grierson, who led black cavalrymen across West Texas in the 1880s, wrote home to Ohio that there were more acres per square mile in West Texas than anywhere else in the world. Even if you live in the shadowy pine forests of East Texas, you know that your state stretches west under open skies all the way to El Paso. The endless country breeds optimism. It seems full of possibilities; any undertaking promises success. Texans tend to be bold optimists.

There is a long-standing debate among historians as to whether Texans are southerners or westerners. The culture of contemporary Texas emerged from

A horse romps in a field of Hill Country wildflowers at the Lyndon B. Johnson National Historical Park in Johnson City. This section preserves Johnson's boyhood home and his grandparents' log cabin settlement. A separate unit north of Lyndon and Lady Bird Johnson's beloved Pedernales River protects the site's working cattle ranch and family cemetery. Nearby a Texas state park devoted to the thirty-sixth president interprets the Sauer-Beckmann Farmstead, a living-history farm presented in its 1918 setting.

three sources: the western cattle kingdom, the southern cotton kingdom, and the oil business. Cattle came first. They were introduced into Texas by the Spanish in the early 1700s, but they did not become economically important until after the Civil War; by then a combination of new technologies made it possible to ship refrigerated beef by rail from slaughterhouses in Chicago to markets in eastern cities. Cattle that were worth three to six dollars a head on the hoof in Texas were suddenly worth thirty to forty dollars a head in Chicago, and there was an unlimited supply of them in Texas. Texans organized a beef industry that, in spite of many changes over the years, is still a major part of our economy. Most male and many female Texans, whether they work on a ranch or in a bank, own a pair of boots, a cowboy hat, and a western belt buckle. You might say it is our state dress. Cattle ranching has left an indelible mark on our way of being and thinking and on our conception of ourselves. Managing cattle on horseback requires skill, patience, and endurance. Ten generations of Texans who have done this have evolved an ethic known as "the cowboy way": finish what you start; take responsibility for what you do; and don't complain. That is the basis of our character.

In the 1850s Texas, newly joined to the Union, became part of the southern cotton kingdom. Our soil was so rich that one settler wrote that "if you put ten-penny nails in the ground you will get a crop of iron bolts." In 1850 Texans produced a mere sixty thousand bales of cotton; ten years later that figure had jumped to nearly half a million bales. Ninety percent of the Texas cotton crop in those years was produced by enslaved African Americans, who made up a third of the state's population.

The Civil War retarded cotton production, but the crop soon recovered. Most of the former slaves became landless tenant farmers, working someone else's land for a share of the crop. But raising cotton as a cash crop proved to be a trap for many Texans. Cash bought clothing, groceries, and small luxuries, but cash-crop farming put small farmers at the mercy of a world cotton market, and when prices fell the farmer who had put all of his land into cotton had nothing to fall back on. His plight was summed up by the ditty, "Ten cent cotton and forty cent meat / How in the world can a poor man eat?" During the 1870s and 1880s, as cotton prices fell drastically, an increasing number of small farmers in Texas lost their farms and joined the former slaves in tenancy. This trend continued into the twentieth century and became a serious social problem. In the 1890s the appearance in Texas cotton fields of the boll weevil, a cotton-destroying insect from Mexico, added to Texas farmers' troubles.

Cotton took a toll on both the land it was grown on and the tenant families who grew it, and reformers urged Texas farmers to diversify their crops and free themselves from enslavement to cotton—"the white scourge." But Texas farmers stuck with cotton for several reasons. It was a crop they knew and understood, having grown it for several generations as their ancestors migrated across the

A calf hangs close to her mother, away from other bawling young ones— it's branding time in the longhorn herd at the Lonesome Pine Ranch near Chappell Hill. The 1,800-acre spread in the rolling hills of Austin County was settled in 1823 by one of Stephen F. Austin's "Old 300," the first Americans in Texas to receive Spanish land grants. Today the ranch maintains one of the nation's largest herds of registered Texas Longhorns.

South. It was a sturdy crop, able to withstand changes in the weather, and its long growing season enabled it to recover from temporary setbacks. Most important, it yielded the highest value per acre of any crop that could be grown in Texas.

Cotton farming for tenant farmers had an annual rhythm that was created by the crop lien system, in which landlords would provide their tenants with enough credit at a rural store to buy seed and tools in the spring and necessities through the summer, with the understanding that the bill would be paid from the proceeds of the tenant's share of the crop in the fall. Of course, crops could fail or be destroyed by rain or hail. If that happened, the annual cycle of indebtedness would start again. That rhythm of debt was burned into the consciousness of several generations of Texans. My great-aunt Bessie, who was born on a Texas tenant farm in the 1880s, eventually became a fairly wealthy woman, with income from several cotton farms as well as oil and gas interests. Until she died in the 1960s, however, she would go every spring to Sakowitz's, Houston's finest department store, to buy her wardrobe and would instruct the clerk, "Now, you tell Mr. Sakowitz I can't pay him until cotton comes in." The clerk would note that she was not to be sent a bill until September.

That hereditary burden of debt has produced a dislike of unnecessary expenditures and a suspicion of showiness that is at the heart of the Texas character. Farming is basically a conservative enterprise, inspiring caution at every step—no farmer wants to take risks with his crop—and the Texan's basic tendency toward conservatism is certainly part our long heritage as cotton farmers.

At the same time, the plight of Texas tenant farmers in the 1870s and 1880s produced a streak of radicalism that is also part of our character, a contrapuntal note to our conservatism. The Farmers' Alliance, founded in Lampasas in 1877 to alleviate the suffering of the tenant farmer, advocated cooperative marketing of cotton and cooperative purchasing of seed and tools. It evolved into the People's Party, a national political movement that placed the blame for the nation's ills on the banking and currency system. The People's Party died out in Texas in the early 1900s, but the idea that a poor person can be robbed with a fountain pen as well as a six-gun is deeply ingrained in many Texans. My father, a professional engineer two generations removed from the cotton patch, liked to tell about the banker with the glass eye. "You could tell which one it was," he would say, "because it was the one with the glint of human kindness in it."

Texas populists elected Ralph Yarborough to the U.S. Senate in 1958 and again in 1964, Ann Richards as governor in 1990, and Wendy Davis to the Texas State Senate in 2008. The movement's ideals are kept alive by the *Texas Observer*, a liberal monthly magazine that has been published in Austin for sixty years. The *Observer* serves as a gadfly to our current conservative majority and has produced such nationally known journalists as Molly Ivins, Willie Morris, Lawrence Goodwyn, and Larry L. King. It is a monthly reminder of the sheer contrariness of some Texans.

After cattle and cotton, the third force that made us who we are was a twentieth-century phenomenon: oil. The gusher at Spindletop, near Beaumont, that rang up the curtain on the petroleum age in Texas came in on January 10, 1901. Over the next thirty years, a series of oil discoveries across the state established petroleum production as Texas's major industry. These finds created legendary boomtowns; places such as Ranger, Desdemona, Eastland, Gladewater, Longview, and Burkburnett still resonate with an older generation of Texans.

The quintessential boom town was Borger, in the Panhandle, laid out in March 1926 on a 240-acre town site by a promoter named Ace Borger. He paid twelve thousand dollars for the site and within six months had sold every lot for a profit of a million dollars. By the next year, forty-five thousand people had come to Borger, including enough gamblers, prostitutes, bootleggers, and dope dealers for it to be known as "Booger Town." So many murders occurred there that the Texas Rangers were sent in to clean it up in 1927; two years later Governor Dan Moody declared martial law for a month and ordered state troops there to enforce it. By 1940 the boom was over and the population had declined to

The Romanesque-style Hopkins County Courthouse in Sulphur Springs is regarded by many as the most beautiful courthouse in Texas. Replete with sandstone trim, stones of contrasting colors, oak woodwork, and romantic touches such as heads embowered in vines, this 1895 civic castle is a masterpiece in a state renowned for its county courthouses. It is the work of the San Antonio architect James Riely Gordon, who designed fifteen courthouses across Texas. When county commissioners suggested replacing the venerable structure in the early 2000s, "preservationists poured from the woodwork," according to one account.

seventeen thousand. Today Borger is still an oil town, with twenty companies listed in the telephone book, and it still retains some of its boomtown atmosphere. Several years ago I was driving down Borger's main street and pulled up at a stoplight next to a mud-covered pickup truck whose door displayed the name of a local oil company. The driver was a beefy man wearing a greasy Stetson. His hands were on the steering wheel, and on one of his fingers was a gold ring studded with at least two dozen diamonds. He was a wildcatter, an independent driller, and that ring was his working capital.

The oil business is characterized by extreme risk and the promise of great rewards. The risk comes not only from the considerable chance of drilling a dry hole while exploring for oil, but also from a failure by companies to provide for new oil reserves while depleting present ones. Industry technology is also rapidly changing, so companies that are not sufficiently flexible fall by the wayside. Success in the oil business is the result of optimism bordering on craziness, individual ingenuity, and a suicidal willingness to take chances. A century of gambling on oil has implanted optimism, individualism, and a love of risk deep into our collective personality as Texans.

Cattle, cotton, and oil created twentieth-century Texas and shaped the character of the Texans I grew up with. But nothing is static. In the year of my birth, 1940, more than half of all Texans still lived in rural areas and we had a colonial economy—we produced raw materials for others to process. Today the vast majority of all Texans live in cities, and a huge portion of our workforce is employed in the manufacturing and service sectors.

World War II brought these changes, stimulating manufacturing in Texas. The petrochemical industry that produced fuel and synthetic rubber along the Gulf Coast grew into the largest of its kind in the world. Shipyards in the same region turned out naval vessels, and huge aircraft plants were built in the Fort Worth–Dallas area. Texans seeking work moved into cities, and the state experienced phenomenal urban growth: Houston expanded by 55 percent between 1940 and 1950, Corpus Christi by 90 percent.

The economic boom initiated by the war has continued, with only a few dips. New industries have spun off from old ones, and new immigrants have arrived, creating millions of new Texans. Asians, for example, are a growing part of our population. Several hundred thousand Indians now live in Texas, most of them in the Dallas and Houston suburbs. Vietnamese is the third most widely spoken language here, after English and Spanish. Dat Nguyen, the son of Vietnamese shrimpers in Rockport, starred as a linebacker for the Dallas Cowboys. You can't get more Texan than that.

Old immigrant populations have also grown. In 1920 people born in Mexico constituted about 5 percent of our population. By 2010 a third of all Texans were Hispanic, and demographers predict that by 2020 Hispanic Texans will be a majority. What this means for the character of Texas is anybody's guess. Perhaps

These boots are made for sellin' at the San Antonio Stock Show and Rodeo. The city even boasts the "World's Largest Cowboy Boots"— urethane-and-steel models standing forty feet tall outside the North Star Mall. Although uncomfortable, high-heeled leather boots with narrow toes that slip easily into stirrups are most suitable for ranchers and cowboys. Custom versions in calfskin, horsehide, and even snakeskin and armadillo skin—with prices starting at six hundred dollars a pair— have become a Texas "boot-scootin'" fashion fixture.

we will become less brash, more gracious, more respectful of our elders, and kinder to our children.

Texas does have blemishes, and lingering racism is one of them. However, the civil rights movement of the 1960s had an enormous impact on the social and economic status of both African Americans and Mexican Americans, and white Texans are becoming increasingly colorblind as one generation succeeds another. Our attitude toward public education is an additional blemish. Texas ranks next to last among the fifty states in the amount of money spent per student on elementary and secondary education. A third problem is the fact that nearly one-fourth of our citizens are without health insurance, the largest percentage of any state in the Union.

"I made the state of Texas," Sam Houston once said, "but I did not make its people, and if they do wrong, the state still remains, in all of its natural beauty, with all of its splendid prospects, varied and delightful." Houston secured Texas's independence from Mexico at the battle of San Jacinto in 1836, served twice as president of the Republic of Texas, and was a U.S. senator from Texas for thirteen years, as well as governor from 1859 to 1861. He was the original Big Texan. A man with a huge ego, a flamboyant dresser—he liked to take his seat on the Senate floor draped in an Indian blanket and wearing a leopard-skin vest— he was a larger-than-life figure. He is commemorated by a larger-than-life concrete statue, sixty-seven feet high, near Huntsville, where he made his last home. The statue can be seen for miles across the flat landscape.

The memory of Sam Houston reminds us that our state was an independent nation for ten years before it became part of the United States, and we treasure the symbols of our former sovereignty, especially our flag, which was also the flag of the Republic of Texas. It is far more ubiquitous than any other state flag, adorning not only state office buildings but also businesses, auto dealerships, and private residences. Texans love to fly it, even if we cannot always remember which stripe goes on top (it's the white one).

The widespread use of the Texas flag, according to the flag historian Robert Mayberry Jr., can be traced to the statewide celebration of the Texas centennial in 1936, an event that made both Texans and the rest of the United States vividly conscious of Texas as a unique place with its own sense of nationhood. The centennial's focal point was the Texas Centennial Exposition in Dallas, which transformed the old state fair grounds at Fair Park into an Art Deco fantasy. The Centennial Exposition was visited by six and a half million Texans, all of whom left with a deeper sense of their history and their identity.

The Texas State Fair is still held every October at Fair Park, now a National Historic Landmark. The fair's most famous attraction, Big Tex, a fifty-five-foot-high talking and gesturing cowboy statue, was added in 1952 as an advertisement for H. D. Lee denim jeans. Big Tex was destroyed by an electrical fire in 2012 but was rebuilt in time for the 2013 state fair.

Encountering this painting of the Texas state flag on a metal barn near Fort Davis in Jeff Davis County should come as no surprise. Lone-star flags, or their creative permutations, are everywhere—on buildings, bumper stickers, advertising signs, and in enormous proportions on auto dealers' flagpoles. They are a ubiquitous symbol of "Texas Pride." The same flag, which got its own Pledge of Allegiance in 1933, was also once the ensign of the sovereign, if short-lived, Republic of Texas.

A fifty-five-foot Big Tex, a sixty-seven-foot Sam Houston—what do these say about us as Texans? Bigness is an essential part of Texas. The Texas historian Randolph Campbell, in his definitive history of the state, *Gone to Texas*, has theorized that the key to Texas's distinctiveness is that our state embodies in an exaggerated way so many of the ideals and emotions shared by all Americans. In this Campbell echoes the title of *The New Yorker* writer John Bainbridge's 1961 book about Texas, *The Super Americans.* To me there is an added ingredient. The spaciousness of our landscape, the magnificent distances between our cities, and the unlimited expanses of our prairies have produced a uniquely expansive way of thinking and acting as Texans.

Carol M. Highsmith's photographs record the grandeur and the variety of the Texas landscape, as well as the vibrant culture that it has produced. She depicts the ornate nineteenth-century courthouses and mansions that cotton prosperity built and the rodeos and *charreadas* and barbecue pits that grew out of our ranching traditions, together with the longhorns and the ranch work that were their foundations. She has photographed the petrochemical industry's barge traffic and the towering skylines of our major cities, and she has caught our individualism with her pictures of some of our more eccentric signs and sculptures—the Light Bulb Shop in Austin, Stanley Marsh III's Cadillac Ranch, and Houston's Orange Show. She has captured the dignity of our state capitol, the beauty of our museums and monuments, and the frivolity of our festivals. Highsmith's photographs will make you proud to be a Texan. If you are not one already, they will make you want to move here and become one.

Texas

Overleaf: It does not look it from the rotunda floor, but the Texas star in the center of the 1888 state capitol dome in Austin is eight feet wide. Opposite: Contractors for the capitol were offered a trade instead of cash payment— three million acres in the Texas Panhandle. The capitol building's architect, Elijah Myers, also designed the Michigan and Colorado statehouses. Below: Stephen F. Austin's portrait hangs behind the lieutenant governor's chair in the Senate chamber.

Above: The 1854 governor's mansion is the oldest continuously inhabited house in Texas. Midway through a renovation, the building was badly damaged in 2008 by a fire started with a Molotov cocktail. Right: The cove molding and mantels with mirrors in the Small Parlor date to the Sayers administration at the turn of the twentieth century. Overleaf: At age eighty, the country singing–songwriting icon Willie Nelson performs with Johnny Depp and other sidemen at Austin's Star of Texas Fair and Rodeo.

Opposite: What goes up on a bucking bronco must come down. Rodeo Austin, which dates to 1938, is the world's fourth-largest indoor pro rodeo, a part of the Star of Texas Fair and Rodeo festivities. Although high school football is more popular, rodeo is the official sport of Texas. Above: The fair's carnival outside the Travis County Expo Center is a feast for the eyes and belly. Pretty-in-pink sisters Samantha and Scarlett Santana are fresh off a spin on the merry-go-round.

Right and opposite: Already synonymous with music and technology, Austin is also an artistic laboratory. Check out the mosaic dude and the car as cactus planter. South Austin, below the Colorado River, is awash in murals, neon inventions, and over-the-top street installations such as these. Below: Tourists will be hard-pressed to get a clear look at the oversized vintage Austin postcard, however. It seems as if just about every visitor to the capital city wants to pose for a selfie in front of it.

Lucy's FRIED CHICKEN

Now Serving
SUNDAY BRUNCH
— 10 - 3 —

000 of gas money in our pockets."
& Courtney, electric vehicle owners

CHARGE FORTH

ARB
AUTO W

Opposite and left: To catch a customer's eye, advertisers in eclectic Austin like to add dashes of whimsy to their messages. No courtly colonel peddles fried chicken at Lucy's place, for example; only a voluptuous bombshell will do here. Not far away, how better to show off a light bulb shop than to suggest the "Eureka!" moment when someone gets a bright idea? Overleaf: Classic beauty abounds in Austin, too, in places such as the downtown Bremond Block of grand Victorian homes. The house built for John Bremond Jr. in 1886 is one of six residences that have been preserved to remember the Bremond family of bankers and merchants. Wrapped in a stunning filigree of cast iron, it is also notable for its crested mansard roof with polychrome slate shingles, a curved front gable, and elaborate dormers.

Opposite: Littlefield Fountain, the sculptor Pompeo Coppini's 1933 memorial to University of Texas students and alumni who died in World War I, bubbles beneath the school's signature Texas Tower from 1937, designed by Paul Philippe Cret. Sadly imprinted in the tower's identity are memories of Charles Whitman's massacre of sixteen people from its heights in 1976. Above: Off campus across the street, Kerry Awn, Rick Turner, and "Tommy B." painted this eccentric mural in 1974 about the tower and much more of Austin.

Above and right: Within the purview of the University of Texas at Austin, but ten miles from campus, the Lady Bird Johnson Wildflower Center protects and displays natural landscapes and more than seven hundred native plants.

Established in 1982 by the former first lady and the actress Helen Hayes, the botanical gardens focus on Mrs. Johnson's interest in conservation of native wildflowers and the environmental benefits of native plant landscaping.

Left and below: Six million bricks went into making Colonel Jesse Driskill's grand Driskill Hotel in downtown Austin in 1886. Its ornamental flourishes include Texas-themed details. The building once featured a ladies' entrance, through which female guests could scurry to their rooms without enduring ungentlemanly comments from the cattlemen in the lobby. Overleaf: More than just water droplets drip in Dripping Springs, west of Austin—so do the juices on the giant grill at the Salt Lick BBQ restaurant, a Texas barbecue institution.

Opposite: President and Mrs. Lyndon B. Johnson returned so often to the modest house on their working ranch in the Texas Hill Country near Johnson City that the little place became known as the Texas White House. Below: Today's National Historical Park grounds there also include ranch meadows, a small farmhouse that was Lyndon Johnson's birth home, and the family cemetery. Johnson's tombstone carries the presidential seal; Claudia Alta "Lady Bird" Johnson's, fittingly, has a flower petal.

Opposite: Trinity Lutheran Church stands directly across the Pedernales River from the LBJ Ranch. Left: The pachyderm relief over the former White Elephant Saloon in Fredericksburg, a German town in the Hill Country, recalls old German drinking halls. Below: The bar in Luckenbach, a dot of a town that was the haunt of Waylon (Jennings), Willie (Nelson), and the boys, is a tourist magnet. Overleaf: Girls have been summering and splashing at Camp Waldemar, near Hunt, since 1926.

Opposite: The ropin' cowpoke on an old cafe sign in Kendall County is ambidextrous—left-handed on this side, right-handed on the other. Above: No one would have trouble spotting the spotted horse near Segovia. Overleaf: San Antonio's lively, subterranean River Walk turned an unsightly slum into an international visitor sensation. A sightseeing barge passes a festive array of restaurant umbrellas en route to a tunnel on the winding San Antonio River.

Left and below: Originally an eighteenth-century Franciscan mission church in San Antonio, the Alamo was destined to become the "Shrine of Texas Liberty." During the so-called Texians' War of Independence in 1835–36, the Alamo's two hundred or so volunteer defenders—the exact number is debated—held out for thirteen days against a Mexican force of thousands before being overwhelmed and slaughtered to the man. At many subsequent victorious battles, the "Texians" shouted "Remember the Alamo!" Today it and its grounds are a National Historical Park.

Opposite and below: San Francisco de la Espada, known today as Mission Espada, was built in San Antonio in the 1750s after Spanish missions in East Texas succumbed to drought, malaria, and French incursions. Here and at other missions throughout the Southwest, Franciscan priests sought to impart the Roman Catholic faith and Spanish ways to native Indians.

Left: Using this labor pool, the Spanish constructed an *acequia* (aqueduct) at Espada to carry water for irrigation and to power a mill.

Right and opposite:
Mission San José y San Miguel
de Aguayo is the largest
of San Antonio's four Spanish
missions. Known as the
Queen of the Missions,
it was almost fully restored
to its original design in the
1930s by Works Projects
Administration laborers.
Spanish missions were not
churches but whole
communities, with the
building as the focal point.
Many structures on the
campus of Texas Tech
University in Lubbock borrow
architectural motifs from
those at Mission San José.

Opposite: The concrete cowboy above the former Kallison's Western Wear store has been a downtown San Antonio icon since the 1940s. Above: A boy cavorts amid a display of Easter blowup figures outside a San Antonio icehouse. Texas icehouses are often makeshift town halls and taverns, not frozen-cube purveyors. Left: An oversized armadillo is a mascot at Bussey's Flea Market, a gathering of merchants in Schertz, a suburb. Outsiders find these leathery mammals adorable. Locals call them "Texas speed bumps."

Fiesta San Antonio is a month-long salute to the city's diverse culture. Right and below: For one event, the Celebration of Traditions Pow-Wow, time-honored American Indian garb is worn by Calvin Osife and Donovan Anderson. Far right: On another night, the water-borne Texas Cavaliers River Parade glides along the River Walk beneath the streets. Overleaf: Twice during Fiesta, young women wearing *ranchera* dresses execute precise movements while riding sidesaddle in an *escaramuza* (mounted skirmish) as part of the Day in Old Mexico rodeo.

Opposite and below: Little Poteet, south of San Antonio, is twice famous: once as the home of the country music star George Strait and again as the venue of a spring strawberry festival. The latter features an old-fashioned small-ring event called the Bad Company Rodeo. You can see what inspired the name. Overleaf: As the gentle Hill Country transitions south and west to scrabblier terrain, wildflowers are edged out by cacti and thorn bushes, alluring in their own right.

Above: Kim and Terry Young recently used hundreds of thousands of pounds of limestone, granite, sand, cement, rock, and block to build Falkenstein Castle, based on unexecuted plans of "Mad King Ludwig" of Bavaria. A residence and an occasional wedding venue, it sits high atop a hill near Burnet. Right: One of the state's natural caverns is the Cave Without a Name near Boerne. Mostly ignored, except by a bootlegger in the 1920s, the cave got its moniker in 1939 when a boy declared it "too beautiful to have one."

Left: He may look like Hopalong Cassidy, but Steve Schmidt, a rancher and retired B-52 bomber pilot, is the sheriff in town at Enchanted Springs Ranch and Old West theme park, special-events venue, and frequent movie and television commercial lot in Boerne. Below: A young visitor, Phallioan Dyson, gets into the Wild West spirit there. And somewhere in these parts, visitors will run into "Pistol-Packin' Paula" Saletnik, whose gun twirling and tossing channels Annie Oakley.

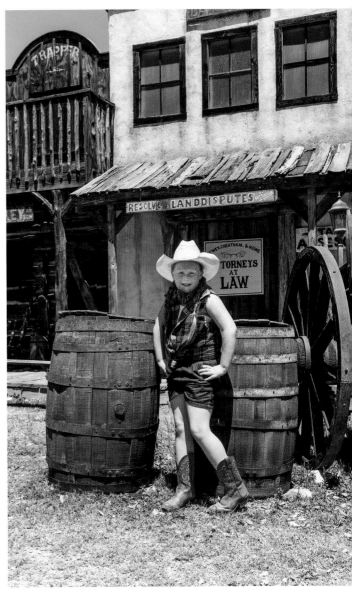

Above: People in a dozen Texas counties often get to bragging that their own profusion of delicate bluebonnet wildflowers is the most stunning and extensive. These beauties are in Kendall County. Opposite: If you guessed that this king and queen of Mardi Gras, James McGroarty and Stella Tedesg, hail from bayou country, think again. They were crowned at the Cowboy Mardi Gras in dusty Bandera. Overleaf: New Braunfels tubers rollick on the Comal River in Prince Solms Park.

Above and opposite: Cloistered in the woods along the Guadalupe River near New Braunfels in Bexar County is a living time machine called Gruene ("Green" to Texans). It is an old German, cooperative cotton town that boomed until the Great Depression and the boll weevil blight of the 1930s sent it slowly spiraling into obscurity. Now heritage tourists flock to relics such as its community buildings and the Victorian Gruene Mansion, with its lacy woodwork and domed tower dating to 1872.

Opposite and above: The rich history of Gonzales, the "Lexington of Texas," is recalled at the Gonzales Pioneer Village Living History Center, which preserves many early buildings, and the Sam Houston Oak, where citizen-soldiers fled overwhelming Mexican forces after the Alamo's fall in San Antonio. Overleaf: St. Mary Catholic Church in little High Hill is considered the queen of Texas's "painted churches." Ferdinand Stockert and Hermann Kern completed the sanctuary's decorative wall and ceiling paintings in 1912.

These pages: Serenity prevails at the Lonesome Pine Ranch near Chappell Hill, where Lars Ellis and his horse, Coyote, ply their arduous yet venerable trade. Overleaf: A study in contrasts—the unremitting energy of sprawling Houston's skyline, captured at dusk—is just sixty miles away.

Houston was a backwater town—an afterthought to Galveston, the state's most prosperous city—until the deadliest hurricane in U.S. history reduced Galveston to splinters in 1900. Below: Methodical dredging of Galveston Bay and Buffalo Bayou produced the Houston Ship Channel, which today carries an unceasing parade of oceangoing vessels and cargo barges to the Gulf of Mexico. Opposite: In a city of glass-and-steel skyscrapers, Houston's 1939 city hall, designed by Joseph Finger, is clad in stolid, sturdy, Texas Cordova limestone.

Left: If visitors were to encounter the artist James Turrell's *Twilight Epiphany* in daytime, they might dismiss it as an intrusive pyramidal pavilion atop a mound on a Rice University campus quadrangle. But the name is prophetic: at sundown it is transformed by a sequence of subtly changing colors into an ethereal space sliver. The 2012 installation is one of Turrell's enclosed "skyspaces," which open to the sky through a roof aperture. Below: Nearby on another campus, the University of St. Thomas, the celebrated architect Philip Johnson in 1997 created the Chapel of St. Basil, which combines cubist, spherical, and linear forms.

Above and opposite: At Houston's Bayou Bend Collection and Gardens, the strictly Texas-made pieces in the Texas Room, including a cowhorn chair, contrast with the classical sculpture of the Roman goddess Diana in the garden. The 1928 property was donated to Houston's citizens by the philanthropist Ima Hogg. Overleaf: Look closely at these longhorn cattle at the Houston Zoo—they are not Texas steers. The prodigious horns of these African Ankole-Watusi can reach up to eight feet from tip to tip.

THE ORANGE SHOW

These pages: Houston's chaotic monuments to artistic expression include gaily festooned "art cars," which parade annually; John Mikovisch's house of forty thousand beer cans; and the Orange Show, Jeff McKissack's wacky paean to the fruit. Overleaf: Colorful reenactments of the seminal Battle of San Jacinto in La Porte do not go any better for the Mexican army than did the original in 1836. And only the real showdown resulted in an independent Republic of Texas and Mexico's loss of one million square miles.

Above: Before the troops advance, visitors to the Battle of San Jacinto restaging are invited to meet reenactors such as Larry Heidbreder, who will beat a hasty retreat with his yoked Texas Longhorns Justice and Liberty once skirmishing ensues. Right: "Terrified townfolk," including the apparently contented brothers Harold Hazeltine Clifford and John Matthew Clifford, will also take cover. Opposite: The reenactment occurs in the shadow of the San Jacinto Monument, at 567 feet the world's tallest monumental column.

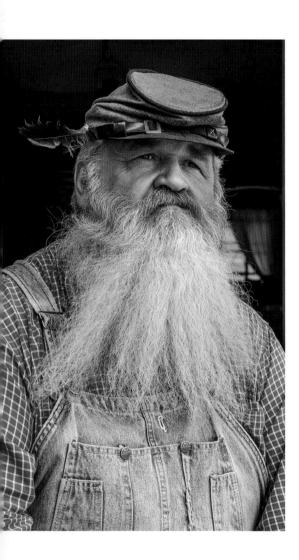

Above and right: The historical interpreter "Uncle Bob" Beringer takes his post at a sharecropper's cabin at the George Ranch Historical Park, a twenty-thousand-acre working ranch in Fort Bend County, southwest of Houston. A living-history partnership of the Fort Bend County Museum Association and the George Foundation, it preserves and interprets the four-generation story of a Texas family, beginning in 1824 and spanning more than a hundred years.

Galveston Island, robust again after a century of deadly hurricanes, is Houston's playground. Below: Seafood and more seafood, touted by an imposing crawfish, is ever-present along Galveston's seawall. Bottom: Hurricane Ike in 2008 demolished Murdoch's Bathhouse, an endearing Galveston institution, but a replacement quickly arose. Right: At the harbor, tall ships such as the *Elissa* provide an everyday flashback. Overleaf: Fish do not steal all the thunder at Galveston's Moody Gardens Aquarium, where a muster of penguins waddles in a dignified sort of way.

Below: In 2008 the ferocious Hurricane Ike and its roiling saltwater surge killed an estimated forty thousand trees. But Donna Leibbert, a member of the Galveston Island Tree Conservancy, recruited chainsaw sculptors to create statues from dead trees in the historic districts. One of them, a wooden geisha with a fan, stands near some handsome Galveston row houses. Right: A larger and more magnificent Galveston architectural allure is the gleaming Sacred Heart Catholic Church, which replaced an even grander church blown to bits by the Great Storm of 1900.

IN HONOREM
SACRATISSIMI
CORDIS JESV
DICATVM
ANNO MCMIII

SACRED HEART
Catholic ☩ Church
• DIOCESE OF GALVESTON-HOUSTON •
~ Masses ~
Saturday: 5:30 p.m.
Sunday: 8:00 a.m., 10:00 a.m.
12:00 Noon &
1:15 p.m. En Español

Above and right: One day in 1901, a gusher at
the Spindletop drilling site spewed "black gold"
150 feet high, spawning a frantic oil rush in the grimy
Gladys City section of what is now Beaumont.
It is all recalled at Lamar University's Spindletop–
Gladys City Boomtown Park, where towers and
stores have been recreated. Overleaf: Things are
more sedate in the breakfast room of the McFaddin-
Ward house museum, reflecting the refined lifestyle
of Beaumont's rich and famous in the early 1900s.

Opposite: This sublime Beaux-Arts parlor of the McFaddin-Ward house accommodated elegant parties thrown by the cattle and oil baron W. P. H. McFaddin and his wife, Ida. These were the glory years that followed Beaumont's Spindletop bonanza—one that hurtled Texas into the forefront of oil exploration and continues to this day. Above: Inside the First Presbyterian Church in Orange, elegance is evident as well. The art-glass dome came from the acclaimed J&R Lamb Studios of New York, a predecessor of Louis Comfort Tiffany's famed glass company.

Below: The sculptor David Adickes's sixty-seven-foot, concrete-and-steel tribute to Sam Houston looms alongside an interstate highway in Huntsville, where the Texas hero retired and died. Right: Eerie bayous are not a Louisiana realm alone. East Texas has its seductive share in Big Thicket National Preserve, a biodiverse ecosystem that includes dense pine forests. Overleaf: An oil barge plies a canal that connects the Sabine Pass waterway—dividing Texas and Louisiana—with the Trinity River, south of Port Arthur.

SAM HOUSTON
1793 - 1863

Left: At Texas A&M University in College Station, Veryl Goodnight's *The Day the Wall Came Down* uses horses, representing freedom, running through the rubble of the Berlin Wall to symbolize the human spirit. The 1996 bronze is outside the George H. W. Bush Presidential Library. Above: Across campus, in front of Kyle Field, stands the Aggies' *Twelfth Man*—the entire, football-rabid student body—portrayed by George E. "Pat" Foley's 1980 statue. In Texas football is king—some of its high school stadiums dwarf their college counterparts.

Left: Bewitching puppets highlight the holdings at the Czech Heritage Museum and Genealogy Center in Temple. Below: A former World War II German prisoner-of-war camp in Hearne displays license plates crafted by detainees. Bottom: A former Waco bottling plant that is now the Dr Pepper Museum displays a vintage ad for the soft drink. Overleaf: Cattle by the thousands, heading for Kansas, were for years driven across what is now this pedestrian bridge over the Brazos River in Waco.

Opposite: Don Hunt's mounted Ranger at the Texas Ranger Hall of Fame and Museum in Waco celebrates America's longest-serving state law-enforcement officers. Above: Along the Brazos River nearby, Robert Summers's sculpture depicts a trail boss herding Texas Longhorns on the old Chisholm Trail. Overleaf: On their ranch near Crawford, President George W. Bush and Laura Bush enjoy their favorite canyon overlook along a rocky trail. Here the former president loves to ride his mountain bike, and Mrs. Bush enjoys scenic hikes.

Below: In Nacogdoches *The Treaty,* a 2003 bronze by Michael Boyett, depicts the moment in 1836 when Sam Houston and other "Texians" fighting for independence secured the agreement of American Indian leaders in East Texas not to join the Mexican forces. Opposite: The ramshackle metal Gatewood-Shelton building in Palestine ("Pallis-teen" to the locals) has served every manner of function since the 1880s—cotton gin, machine shop, trading post, antiques store, and, most recently, a music club.

Left: A 1950s-vintage hardware truck suits Jefferson, a picturesque East Texas town. Almost every commercial building on its main street has earned a historical marker. Above: The name of Jefferson's 1872 House of the Seasons derives from the play of light through its cupola's stained-glass windows, which produces effects that suggest all four seasons. Overleaf: Recalling the oil bonanza of the 1930s, the East Texas Oil Museum in Kilgore has created a graphically mucky "Boomtown U.S.A."

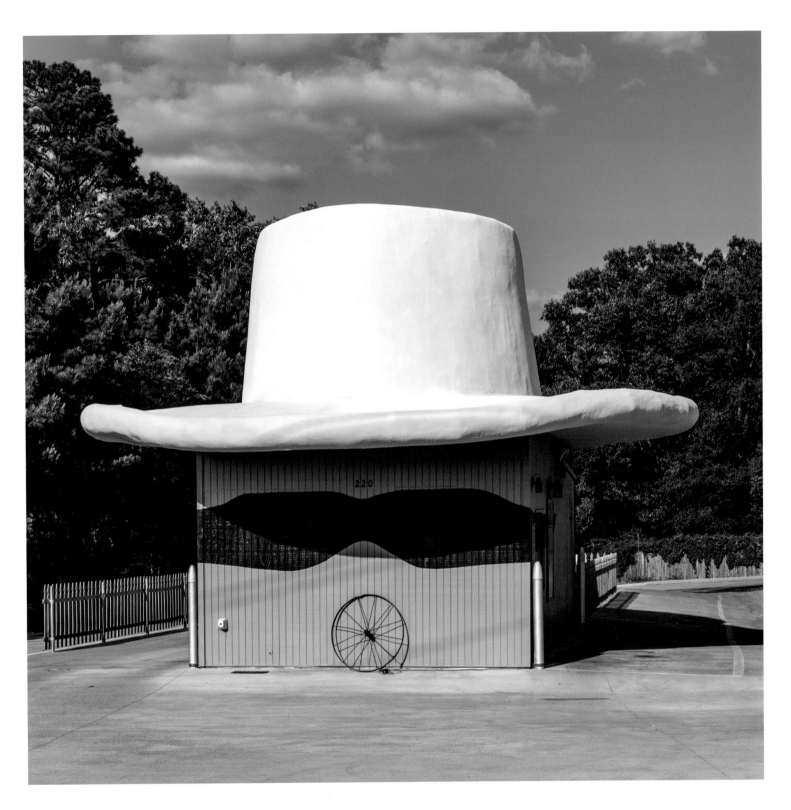

Opposite: The Kilgore College Rangerettes—
the high-kicking, splits-jumping, precision-dancing
choreography team that got its start in 1939—
have performed on four continents. They bring
show business to the gridiron at the small
East Texas college as well as at Dallas Cowboys

professional football games and the annual
Cotton Bowl college contest. Above: In nearby
Tyler, a Kickerz Coffee drive-through store
imaginatively interprets the masked Lone
Ranger of comics, radio, and television fame.
There is no sign of Tonto, however.

Ranching still thrives across much of Texas, but many owners brood that they will be the last generation. Right: A pair of spotted donkeys in Titus County seem to say, "Like mother, like son." Below: At the entrance to another ranch, in Delta County, a sinewy, synthetic stallion steals the show. Opposite: Denton County has a newer courthouse, but its 1896 Romanesque-style "Courthouse-on-the-Square" remains in full use as, among other things, a historical museum.

Left and below: Texarkana, in the state's northeast corner, is a divided town—half lies across State Line Avenue in Arkansas. But the elegant Perot Theatre, with its golden and blue classical decor, has been everybody's destination for stage and film entertainment since 1924, when it opened as the Saenger chain's "Gateway to the West." The theater's name changed after the native son H. Ross Perot contributed much of the funding for a head-to-toe restoration in 1979.

In Texas cowboy hats can be found in more places than just on the heads of ranch hands and urban cowpokes. Below: Even the 1973 Eiffel Tower in Paris . . . Texas wears one. When Tennessee added ten feet to its twin tower, Lone Star boosters placed a saucy red chapeau on their own. Right: Another hat tops the head of the acclaimed country music star Clint Black, a Texan since age one. He was in McKinney for a music video filming.

Above: *The Hiker,* Theo Alice Ruggles Kitson's 1928 statue to Spanish-American War veterans, rests outside the Municipal Auditorium in Wichita Falls. Right: All is quiet as dusk settles on a freight yard and a grain elevator there. Overleaf: Among the familiar features of the Dallas skyline are the illuminated sky ball of the 1978 Reunion observation tower and the green neon outline of the 1985 Bank of America Plaza tower, at seventy-two stories the city's tallest structure.

Opposite: The former Dallas County Courthouse, built in 1892 of red sandstone with rusticated marble accents— and fondly known as the "Old Red Courthouse"—is now a museum. Above: In close-by Pioneer Park, Robert Summers's seventy larger-than-life bronze steers re-create long-ago cattle drives on the Shawnee Trail, the easternmost route along which Texas Longhorns were herded to northern railheads. Left: A replica of the 1841 log home and trading post of Dallas's founder, John Neely Bryan, sits in Dealey Plaza.

Below and right: On November 22, 1963, Lee Harvey Oswald, the presumed—by most—assassin of President John F. Kennedy, found a perch above Dealey Plaza in a sixth-floor storeroom of the Texas School Book Depository in Dallas. The site is now the Sixth Floor Museum, run by the nonprofit Dallas County Historical Foundation. Among the museum's exhibits are the tan suit and orange shoes worn by Jim Leavelle, the detective who was escorting Oswald when he was shot and mortally wounded two days later.

Above photographs: The decaying Old East Dallas industrial neighborhood called Deep Ellum—residents' corruption of Deep Elm—has become one big artistic workshop. Right: *The Eye,* Tony Tasset's thirty-foot-tall oculus does its staring downtown, but it would be at home in Deep Ellum. Opposite: A series of stainless-steel *Traveling Man* sculptures have one foot planted in Deep Ellum and the other in the future. Overleaf: The architect Philip Johnson's Glory Window unfolds in the spiraling 1976 Chapel of Thanksgiving, part of the city's Thanks-Giving Square.

Below and right: Called the "World of Wonder" by the *Dallas Morning News*, the Perot Museum of Nature and Science was first housed at the site of the 1936 Texas Centennial Exposition. In 2012 its principal collection was moved to a dramatic new building at Victory Park designed by Thom Mayne of Morphosis, a Pritzker Architecture Prize winner. Escalators move through the canted glass protrusion. One of the ten permanent exhibit venues, the Lyda Hill Gems and Minerals Hall, displays rare jewels and geodes, some of them enormous.

PEROT MUSEUM OF NATURE AND SCIENCE

FOUNDING DONORS
THE PEROT FAMILY
LYDA HILL
JAN AND TREVOR REES-JONES
SALLY AND FORREST HOGLUND

Opposite: This sinuous cable bridge over the Trinity River in Dallas, designed by the daring Spanish architect Santiago Calatrava, opened in 2010. It is named after Margaret Hunt Hill, a Dallas philanthropist who was the daughter of the legendary Texas oil entrepreneur H. L. Hunt. When lighted, its forty-story center support arch can be seen miles away. Below: Barbara Hepworth's 1963 bronze, *Squares with Two Circles,* is a fixture at the Nasher Sculpture Center in the Dallas Arts District.

Left: At the "Texanic"-style Centennial Hall in Dallas's Fair Park, site of the 1936 Texas Centennial Exposition, a statue represents Spanish rule. Above: A more whimsical figure from the fair, the *Texas Woofus,* has been re-created there. According to its sculptor, Lawrence Tenney Stevens, the woofus combines long, wavy cattle horns, a sheep's head and neck flap, a stallion's neck and mane, a hog's body, turkey tail feathers, and duck wings. The fate of the original *Woofus* is a mystery.

Above: Texas Star, the 212-foot Ferris wheel that supplies a bird's-eye view of the Texas State Fair in Dallas each fall, is the largest in North America. Opposite: A more genial staple is Big Tex, the gigantic cultural icon that has reigned at the fair since 1952. Although a rambunctious newcomer debuted in 2013 after the previous, much-adored Tex burned to a crisp in an electrical fire the previous autumn, this view shows his dearly departed predecessor.

Above: When the exclusive Highland Park Village in Dallas opened in 1931, the Spanish Colonial–themed retail mall became America's first enclosed shopping center. Right: That's Mount Vernon, all right. But it is Texas's Mount Vernon—an outsized facsimile of George Washington's Virginia estate, once occupied by the oilman H. L. Hunt. Unlike Washington's comparatively cramped abode, this version on Dallas's White Rock Lake includes a pool and a pool house, a four-lane bowling alley, lighted tennis courts, a sixteen-car garage, and putting greens.

Above and right: Opened in
1984, the Dallas Arboretum
and Botanical Garden offers
sixty-six acres filled with
varied landscapes that appeal
to garden lovers of all species,
children included. Scattered
throughout are serene ponds
and contrasting sculptures,
as well as plenty of plants to
ponder. Opposite: Working
with Oglesby Greene
Architects, Edward Baum and
John Maruszczak designed
the 2001 Dallas Police
Memorial downtown. Light
filters through fallen officers'
badge numbers in the
stainless-steel shelter to
stencil the numbers below.

Below: The final concert by the "King of Country," George Strait, at Arlington's AT&T Stadium in 2014 broke the Rolling Stones' 1981 record for the largest indoor crowd in North America. Bottom: Jerry Jones, owner of the NFL Dallas Cowboys, joins his wife, Gene, on the field in the cavernous stadium that some call "Jerry World." Right: Team officials say many in the crowd watch the entire game on the stadium's 160-foot-wide video screen, rather than on the field. Overleaf: The Fort Worth Stockyards' twice-daily running of the bulls is more a stroll for the Texas Longhorns.

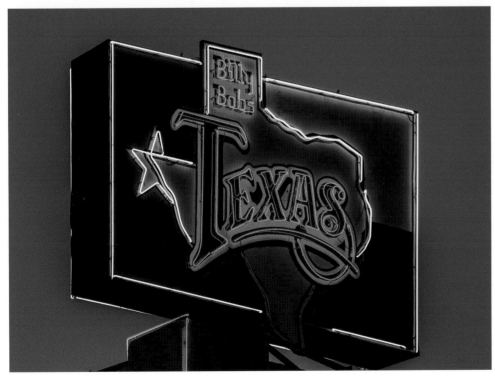

These pages: Dusk in Fort Worth brings out the best, or the most imaginative, street and advertising art. A lot of it adopts a reliable Old West motif. Perhaps the half-invisible cowpuncher should be called "The Sundown Kid." Overleaf: Twilight also flatters the Modern Art Museum of Fort Worth in the city's Cultural District. Designed by the noted Japanese architect Tadao Ando and opened in 2002, the building features five long pavilions set into a reflecting pond.

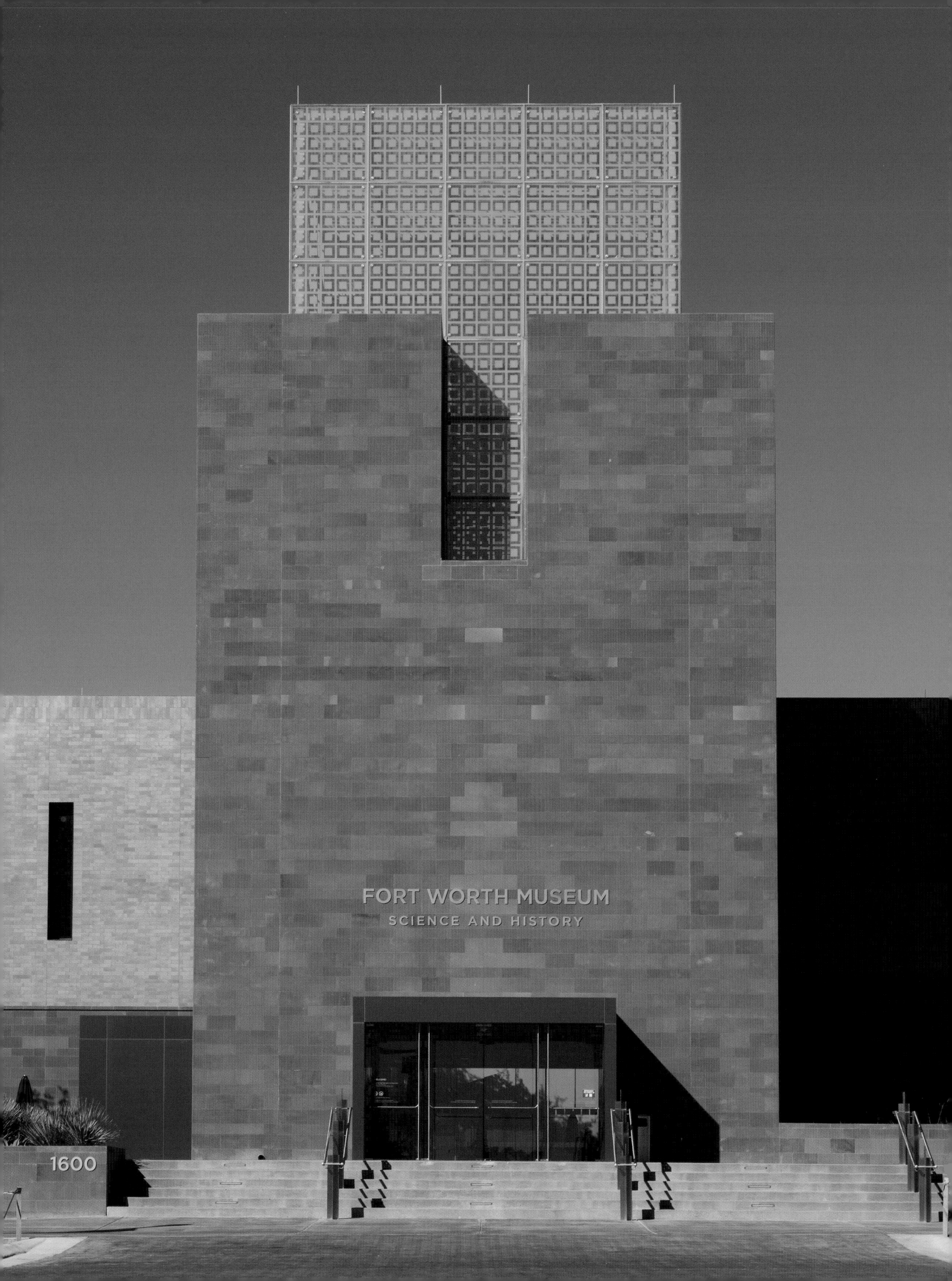
FORT WORTH MUSEUM
SCIENCE AND HISTORY
1600

To go with its cowboy chic, Fort Worth offers plenty of culture and evocative architecture. Opposite: The Fort Worth Museum of Science and History started life as a children's museum, but its mission and name evolved. Its latest building, from 2009, was designed by the architects Legorreta + Legorreta with Gideon Toal and features a planetarium and an IMAX dome. Left: Symphony and opera halls sometimes announce their productions with tasteful gongs. But at Fort Worth's Bass Performance Hall, two angels sculpted by Marton Varo sound mighty trumpets, metaphorically. Designed by David M. Schwarz and opened in 1998, the hall follows the model of classic European opera houses and welcomes the symphony, opera, ballet, Broadway shows, and similar musical events.

Below: Horses, or at least one of them, get their due in Fort Worth at a fountain on the Old Courthouse lawn. When it was dedicated in 1892, the watering place served as a trough for the city's nags. Right: The Chisholm Trail, along which hundreds of thousands of longhorns were driven from South Texas to a Kansas railhead after the Civil War, established Fort Worth as "Cowtown." These cattle drives come to life above Sundance Square in Richard Haas's three-story trompe l'oeil mural from 1988.

1867 CHISH

Opposite: Jack Maxwell's 2006 *Jacob's Dream* at Abilene Christian University in Abilene illustrates the biblical account of the dream. Below: In small towns across the state, the most popular name for theaters, unsurprisingly, is Texas or Texan, including this snappy little one in Bronte in Coke County. Open on and off since the 1940s, the theater is now used for community events rather than first-run movies—even Westerns. But it may not yet have screened its "last picture show."

Top: The cowhand-chef sign atop Sweetwater's Nolan County Coliseum gives an inkling that the grub must be good. Above: Down the street, the Palomino Hotel's marquee makes one want to hop in the old Woodie and head west. Right: Sweetwater is best known for the Jaycees' annual "World's Largest Rattlesnake Roundup." Here Miss Snake Charmer, Hannah Smith, and the cowboy serpent handler, Terry "Hollywood" Armstrong, hoist a hefty specimen that later may have starred at the fried-snake barbecue booth.

Right: It is doubtful that Coke is any longer "served here," inside an old brick building in San Angelo. Below: There is probably not much smithing downtown anymore, despite Crystal Goodman's evocative mural on a building that contained Vogel's Blacksmith Shop starting in 1929. Opposite: Both the thousands of sheepherders in the area and Leonardo da Vinci would approve of the decorative sheep nearby. Two dozen local artists embellished the un-ewes-ual fiberglass sculptures in 2007.

Mostly just for the fun of it, owners of old Texas gasoline stations that flourished during the heyday of the open road in Gonzales and Athens and El Paso and elsewhere have restored them to their halcyon stylishness. Opposite: The Panhandle city of Shamrock on historic Route 66 refurbished the Conoco Tower and the adjacent U Drop Inn Cafe. Above and left: Franklin Bryant and Lynn Fuller gussied up the full-service Sinclair station in Snyder, right down to the "ding-ding" alert hose.

Above and right: Inside
a bunkhouse, Annie Young
Shelton and Ferol Shelton,
managing owners of the
vast RO cattle ranch near
Clarendon in the Panhandle,
display some of their
Old West accoutrements.
Opposite: Up a ways in
Groom, a water tower that
once supplied a truck stop
lists a tad. No tornado
or earthquake caused the tilt—
it was a deliberate marketing
ploy to lure customers off
Route 66. Overleaf: Thunder-
clouds and their deluges
and hail pelterings are regular
visitors to the Panhandle.

Left: Graffiti artists are not just tolerated at the Cadillac Ranch art installation near Amarillo—they are encouraged to change the look of the ten 1949–63 Caddies every day if they like. The display was commissioned by Stanley Marsh III, an eccentric helium tycoon, and executed by a San Francisco design firm named the Ant Farm. Above: A close look at the neon marquee discloses that it does not announce a theater. It is, instead, an unconventional bank adornment.

Opposite: Billboards for the Big Texan Steak Ranch on Route 66 in Amarillo often extol its "free" seventy-two-ounce steaks. But to get the meat—the size of a small roast—gratis, the diner must finish it and several trimmings in an hour. Many try; most fail. Above and left: Multiple variations of Route 66 signs can be seen across the Panhandle. Overleaf: McLean has a museum devoted to the Mother Road, as well as, curiously, the history of barbed wire.

Above: The Phillips 66 regional gasoline empire got
its start in Oklahoma. It arrived in Texas in 1928 in the
little Panhandle town of McLean, where the first
station, now owned by the Texas Route 66 Association,
is a landmark. Across the state are similar little pitched-
roof buildings carrying the letter *P*. Many of them were
once retail outlets for Pure, not Phillips 66. Opposite:
A windmill near Pampa waits for a zephyr or two.

Right: The deteriorating, forty-seven-foot-tall Tex Randall in the city of Canyon once casually clasped a giant cigarette in his right hand. Below: More than seventy-five Texas cattle brands and a longhorn detail greet visitors to Canyon's Panhandle-Plains Historical Museum. Opposite: In Palo Duro Canyon State Park, the nation's second-largest gorge, Paul Lundergreen rides his horse, Ghost, high above a rocky amphitheater to open the musical drama *Texas*. Overleaf: Palo Duro's signature formation is the Lighthouse spire to the right.

Opposite: A mountain biker tests the trail in Palo Duro Canyon, where summertime temperatures routinely eclipse 100 degrees and hikers are cautioned to carry beaucoup water. Above: To the south in Plainview, the nexus of the Panhandle's cotton patch, a massive elevator dominates the landscape. Left: Nearby Lubbock is an agricultural town, too, but with an artistic flair. Robert Bruno, an architect and sculptor, spent twenty-three years building his unusual home there from 110 tons of steel.

Opposite: A statue of Buddy Holly anchors the West Texas Walk of Fame in Holly's hometown of Lubbock. Across the street, a museum unfolds the life story of the rock-'n'-roll legend, born Charles Hardin Holley, who was killed in a 1959 plane crash. A Lubbock street is even named for Holly's band, the Crickets, who were not aboard. Above: Out in the country in tiny Wink, another rock superstar, Roy Orbison, is honored with a tiny museum and a contemplative mural.

Right: Beauty is in the eye of the beholder in remote West Texas, but for many passersby, rough-hewn places such as Sooky's Bar in Van Horn hold considerable charm. Below: In little Marathon, the luxurious Gage Hotel stands out. This 1927 adobe was designed by the architect and engineer Henry Trost, whose work includes hundreds of buildings across the Southwest, including the El Capitan Hotel in Van Horn. Opposite: Less known in Marathon is the Big Hair Shop, where presumably big hair is optional.

Opposite: One of the most fascinating destinations in Texas is Hueco Tanks State Park, east of El Paso. The park's main allure is its series of exceptional, expressive pictographs. Access to the prime samples, such as this drawing, is restricted because some have been defaced by thoughtless graffiti taggers. Above: The tanks themselves are not metallic or cylindrical—they are natural rock depressions, where collected water sustained ancient cultures and hardy newcomers in the grim and isolated high desert.

Right and below: El Paso's Nuestra Señora de la Concepción del Socorro, or Socorro Mission, in 1840 replaced an earlier Franciscan mission. Serving Piro, Tano, and Jamez Indians who had fled New Mexico during the Pueblo Revolt, that mission was destroyed by a flood of the Rio Grande. Opposite: Not far away, a dramatic statue introduces the Tigua Indian Cultural Center at the Ysleta del Sur Pueblo, which celebrates more than three centuries of tribal history in El Paso.

Opposite and above: The oldest mission in Texas, now run by the Catholic Diocese of El Paso, is the San Ysleta Mission church. It was built in 1682 by the Tigua tribe, which had been forced from its ancestral home near what is now Albuquerque, New Mexico. Left: A complementary mural is painted on the wall of a building across from the church. Unlike California's twenty-one Spanish missions, which form a coherent mission trail, many Texas missions have come and gone and moved locations.

Opposite: The 1789 grotto and chapel in tiny San Elizario are often mistaken for a Spanish mission, as they are close to two in El Paso. The church, however, is an example of late adobe architecture of the Spanish colonial period. Above: The nearby community of Fabens is even smaller than San Elizario, but it also boasts a beautiful place of worship— Our Lady of Guadalupe Catholic Church.
Overleaf: Montana Street runs from the heart of El Paso into the desert, where the sunsets are striking.

Right: The entry sign for an adobe vacation rental in Marfa gives no hint that this dusty town has morphed into an applauded center of modernist art. Below: The minimalist artist Donald Judd's boxlike *Judd's Cubes* from 1980–84 dot the grounds of the Chinati Foundation, a contemporary art museum. Opposite: In little Valentine, the sculptors Michael Elmgreen and Ingar Dragset installed a head-turning Prada store knockoff neither to be used nor repaired, so that it might slowly degrade back into the sere landscape.

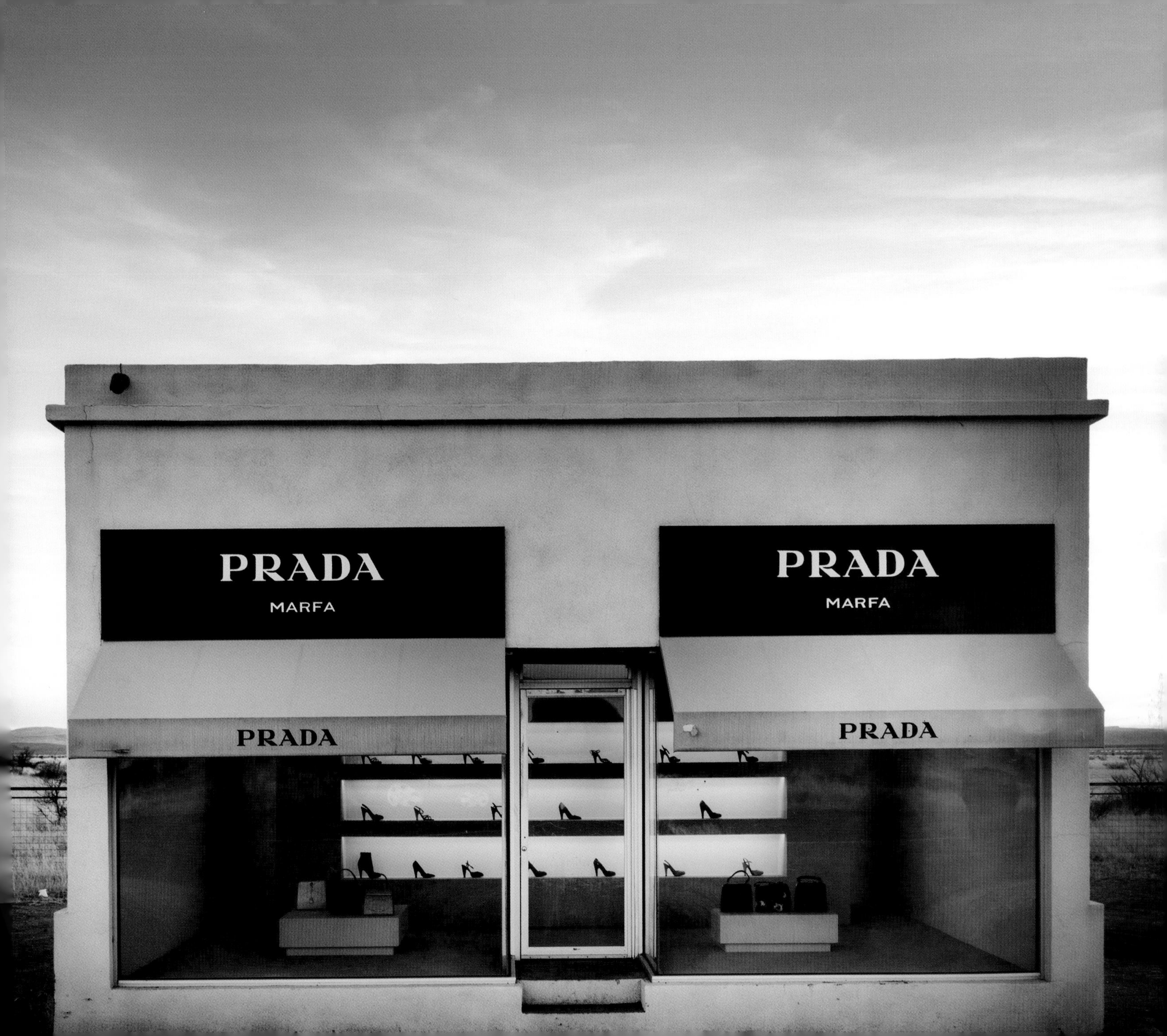
PRADA
MARFA
PRADA
MARFA
PRADA
PRADA

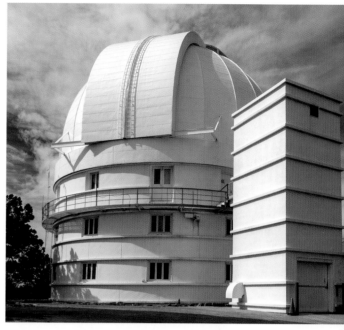

Left: Fort Davis, a little town in Jeff Davis County, is the site of a National Historic Site that protects one of the best remaining examples of U.S. Army forts in the Southwest. Top and above: Also found here are numerous sky-watching stations at the McDonald Observatory, managed by the University of Texas at Austin. Its eighty-two-inch-wide Otto Struve Telescope, constructed between 1933 and 1939, was the second-largest in the world at the time.

Above and right: The theater and a clever crossing sign are vestiges of Terlingua, a hardscrabble, recently reviving Big Bend Country settlement. Far right: Why is James Dean depicted in Stylle Read's mural outside the Reata Restaurant in Alpine? Out of view is the Reata Mansion, which starred in Dean's classic movie *Giant*, filmed twenty-five miles away in 1956. Overleaf: This now abandoned Western movie set in Big Bend Ranch State Park was used in several films and music videos.

Below: The waters of the Rio Grande, separating Mexico and the United States, seem to vanish into the cliffs that abut them in Big Bend National Park. Right: On temperate days, people come to kayak or to examine and skip stones in the area. Overleaf: The meandering waters of the Amistad National Recreation Area, outside Del Rio, are a popular fishing and boating destination. The reservoir was created in 1969 by the Amistad Dam across the Rio Grande from the Mexican city of Ciudad Acuña.

Left: Laredo, a transportation funnel into and out of Mexico, is the largest inland port on the United States–Mexican border. It began as a single villa, and today plenty of fetching successors remain, such as the one behind these walls. The original compound, just across San Agustin Plaza, served as the capital of the brief Mexican Republic of the Rio Grande in 1840. Above: In the plaza is a statue of Saint Augustine, patron saint of Laredo, erected in 1969 thanks to public contributions.

Above and opposite: Want to meet some sort-of-real, kind-of-scary desperados, such as Carlos Lara of the Los Liberadores, who is flanked, opposite, by Pablo Martinez and Javier Rodriguez? Catch the Zapata County Fair, where they busy themselves making an intimidating impression. Visitors can try some goat meat, eat all the jalapeños they can handle, bake something, compete in the tight-jeans contest, or try their hand at *grito*, which is the Mexican equivalent of shouting "Yahoo!" or "Yeehaw!" at a hoedown.

Above: Most towns build monuments to their heroes. But little Hidalgo, where the country's first killer bee colony was found, took a more mirthful approach. In 1992 it built the *World's Largest Killer Bee*, sculpted by Jerome Vettrus, and it even promotes itself as the "Killer Bee Capital"—

not just of America but of the world. The insect, built largely of fiberglass over steel, is as threatening as the real, invasive, ill-tempered variety. Opposite: In South Texas, just about everything, including this refreshment stand in Escobares, is colorful.

All manner of lovely little churches are tucked away throughout South Texas. Below: Our Lady of Lourdes Grotto in Rio Grande City was built of local rocks and petrified wood to resemble the shrine at Lourdes in the south of France. Right: Shepherded by the Diocese of Brownsville, the faith community of San Miguel Arcangel, or Saint Michael the Archangel ("Prince of All Angels"), in Los Ebanos assembles right next to the Rio Grande.

Left: A cemetery is probably not exactly "festive," but this one in Los Ebanos—and others like it throughout the Rio Grande valley—are certainly vibrant. Below: Just down the street is a ferry that crosses into Mexico and back. That by itself is hardly unusual. But this little one is El Chalán, the last hand-pulled, cable-guided, pedestrian and two- or three-car ferry of its kind on the long river. The multifaceted ferry station sign exaggerates its significance a tad.

Los Ebanos · 241

Opposite and above: There really is a Havana, Texas, represented radiantly by its principal taco stand. But, as the saying goes, if you blink along U.S. 83, you'll miss it. The designation can be traced to the Cuban capital, after which the original Spanish land-grant holder named the town in 1767. Overleaf: Quinta Mazatlan ("Country House in the Land of the Deer") is a city-owned historic adobe mansion within a nature and birding center in McAllen.

Right: The startling, vaguely anthropomorphic *Wings of the City* statue temporarily exhibited outside the Brownsville Museum of Fine Art was created by the Mexican artist Jorge Marín in 2010. Below: By design there is a gap in the United States–Mexican border-security fence. It allows U.S. travelers to visit the Rabb Plantation, part of the Sabal Palm Sanctuary along the Rio Grande. The fence and its void are heavily patrolled. Opposite: An elaborate fountain created in 1850 graces Brownsville's Market Square.

Below: Giraffes such as this fellow at Brownsville's Gladys Porter Zoo are (a) tall, (b) not the greatest lookers, and (c) terribly curious, when they are not being pursued by cheetahs. The bony knobs between his ears protect him in a fight, so giraffes are also, occasionally, (d) grouchy. Right: Sea turtles, including this handsome specimen at the Texas State Aquarium in Corpus Christi, can be, well, snappish. This guy or gal is not frowning, however; it looks that way all the time.

Right: The Point Isabel Lighthouse was built in 1852 to guide ships through the Brazos Santiago Pass. Confederate and Union soldiers occupied it in turn during the Civil War. The beacon often stood dark over the years, until the Texas State Park Board restored it with a lamp, but not its powerful lens, in 1952. Opposite: Across the street in Port Isabel stands the Champion Building, an 1899 store on which a local— reputedly one-armed!—man painted an encyclopedic mural about fish.

Opposite and above: Goliad, the city where Mexican forces executed many Texan soldiers who had surrendered during the Texas War of Independence in 1835–36, has become a pilgrimage site. The town includes the sumptuous Spanish colonial–era mission Nuestra Señora del Espíritu, reconstructed by the Civilian Conservation Corps in the 1930s. Overleaf: Also here is the Presidio La Bahía, which the Mexicans overwhelmed. Outside the fort fly nine flags of entities that have ruled Texas territory or fought over the Goliad site.

First edition published in 2014 by
Chelsea Publishing, Inc.
7501 Carroll Avenue, Takoma Park, Maryland 20912
800-847-6918

Publication made possible through the generous
support of Lyda Hill

Photographs from the Carol M. Highsmith Archive
of the Library of Congress

www.CarolHighsmithAmerica.com
www.ThisisAmericaFoundation.org

ISBN 978-1-4951-2463-1

Design and typography by Robert L. Wiser
Composed in Hoefler text and titling
Photograph captions by Ted Landphair
Production by Diane Maddex, Archetype Press
Printed by Tien Wah Press in Singapore

Front endpapers:

Wary longhorn steers and calves take to running on the
Lonesome Pine Ranch near Chappell Hill in Austin County.

A metal-art cowboy doffs his hat along the road between
Johnson City and Kerrville.

Back endpapers:

A longhorn blends nicely into the background of a mound
in Terlingua, near Big Bend National Park.

Texans are wild about wildflowers such as this array in the
Hill Country, about which they are wild, too.